Friendship is a gift, a treasure to hold
A bond that grows stronger, as time unfolds
It's built on trust, and a love so true
A shoulder to lean on, when skies are blue

Friends share laughs, and memories so sweet
In good times and bad, their friendship complete
A hand to hold, when the road is rough
A source of support, when things get tough

Friends stand by each other, through thick and thin
Lifting each other, when the going gets grim
They light up our lives, with their joy and cheer
Bringing us sunshine, year after year

So here's to friendship, a bond so strong
May it last forever, and never do wrong
For a true friend is a gift beyond measure
A treasure to keep, beyond all measure.

Friends are the stars, that light up the night
Guiding us forward, shining so bright
They bring laughter, and wipe away tears
Filling our lives, with love and good cheer

A true friend listens, without any judgment
Offering a kind word, with a gentle touch
Their laughter is contagious, spreading good cheer
Bringing joy to all those, who hold them dear

Friends are the sun, on a cloudy day
Warming our hearts, in every way
Their gentle support, makes all things right
Shining a light, on our darkest night

So here's to friendship, a bond so true
A treasure beyond measure, that shines through
For a true friend is a gift from above
A source of happiness, and a symbol of love.

Friendship is a journey, that takes us through life
Filled with laughter, and moments of strife
It's a bond that grows stronger, with every step
Built on trust, and a love that won't bend

Friends are the rain, that nourishes the soul
Giving us strength, to reach our goal
They lift us up, when we are feeling low
And show us the way, when the road ahead is unknown

Friends are the fire, that warms our hearts
Bringing comfort, and a sense of peace to our parts
Their love and support, helps us to grow
Shining a light, in our hearts aglow

So here's to friendship, a bond so rare
A treasure that lasts, beyond compare
For a true friend is a gift of gold
A blessing to have, worth more than gold.

Friendship is a bond, that ties two hearts as one
Built on trust, and a love that's never done
It's laughter and tears, shared hand in hand
A journey together, through life's shifting sands

Friends are the light, that guides us on our way
Lifting us up, when we stumble and sway
They bring us comfort, when the world gets rough
And remind us of love, when things get tough

Friends are the stars, that shine so bright
Filling our lives, with their guiding light
They bring joy and laughter, to brighten our days
And help us find hope, in the darkest of ways

So here's to friendship, a bond so true
A treasure beyond measure, that shines through
For a friend is a gift, from the heavens above
A source of happiness, and a symbol of love.

Friendship is a rose, that blooms with grace
Nourished by love, it grows in its place
It's the laughter and smiles, shared hand in hand
A bond that endures, through life's shifting sands

Friends are the sunshine, that warms the soul
Bringing peace and comfort, and making us whole
They lift us up, when we fall to the ground
And stand by us, when the world brings us down

Friends are the wind, that carries us high
Helping us soar, to reach for the sky
Their laughter and love, lifts our spirits up
Bringing hope and joy, to every cup

So here's to friendship, a bond so rare
A treasure that lasts, beyond compare
For a friend is a gift, from the heart of the sun
A blessing to have, when our journey is done.

Friendship is a song, that echoes through time
A melody of love, that will always rhyme
It's the laughter and jokes, shared hand in hand
A bond that endures, through life's shifting sands

Friends are the rainbow, after a stormy day
Bringing color and light, to chase the blues away
They offer a smile, when tears fall like rain
And hold our hand, when we face life's pain

Friends are the waves, that gently roll in
Bringing comfort and peace, and washing away sin
Their laughter and love, washes over us like tide
Leaving us feeling, happy and full inside

So here's to friendship, a bond so pure
A treasure that shines, forevermore
For a friend is a gift, from the heart of the sea
A blessing to have, throughout eternity.

When life gets tough, and the road is steep
And the weight of the world, begins to creep
We need friends, to help us through
To offer a hand, and see us through

Friends are the light, that shines so bright
Guiding us forward, through the darkest night
They bring laughter and joy, to chase away pain
And offer a shoulder, to ease the strain

When our hearts are heavy, and our spirits low
Friends are the sunshine, that helps us grow
Their love and support, helps us to stand
Lifting us up, and taking us by the hand

So here's to friends, a treasure so true
A bond that endures, and shines like the dew
For a friend is a gift, from the heavens above
A source of happiness, and a symbol of love.

When life becomes a storm, and the winds blow strong
And we feel like we're lost, and don't belong
We need friends, to hold our hand
To help us weather, this difficult land

Friends are the anchors, that keep us steady
Their love and support, makes us ready
For the challenges life, may have in store
Their presence, helps us endure

When our hearts are breaking, and we're filled with doubt
Friends are the rays of light, that help us out
Their laughter and love, helps us to mend
And together, we find peace at the end

So here's to friends, a treasure so rare
A bond that lasts, beyond compare
For a friend is a gift, from the heart of the sun
A blessing to have, when our journey is done.

When life becomes a maze, and the path is unclear
And we're searching for direction, with no one near
We need friends, to show us the way
To help us navigate, through this troublesome day

Friends are the candles, that light our path
Their love and guidance, helps us to laugh
At the obstacles life, may place in our way
Their presence, helps us face the day

When we're feeling lost, and we're all alone
Friends are the stars, that help us find our way home
Their laughter and love, helps us to see
That together, we can conquer anything

So here's to friends, a bond so bright
A treasure that shines, through the darkest night
For a friend is a gift, from the heart of the sky
A blessing to have, until the day we die.

A good friend is someone, who brings a smile to your face
Who makes you feel special, with their warm embrace
They're always there for you, through thick and thin
A constant companion, until the very end

A good friend is honest, and tells you like it is
Their words of wisdom, a priceless gift to give
They offer a listening ear, and a heart that understands
A source of comfort, in a world that often demands

A good friend is kind, and gives without a thought
Their generosity, a treasure that cannot be bought
They lift you up, when you're feeling low
And stand by you, through the highs and the lows

So here's to good friends, a rare and precious find
A bond that lasts, a love that's one of a kind
For a good friend is a gift, from the heart of the sun
A blessing to have, when our journey is done.

A good friend is someone, who walks beside you
Offering a hand, to help you make it through
They listen with their heart, and understand
A constant companion, in a shifting land

A good friend is loyal, and always there
Their love and support, a treasure beyond compare
They lift you up, when you're feeling down
And bring you joy, when life wears you out

A good friend is honest, and always speaks the truth
Their words of wisdom, a guiding light for you
They offer a shoulder, to ease the pain
And help you find happiness, again and again

So here's to good friends, a bond so rare
A treasure that shines, beyond compare
For a good friend is a gift, from the heart of the sky
A blessing to have, until the day we die.

A good friend is someone, who stands by your side
A constant companion, through life's ebb and tide
They offer a smile, when the world is rough
And help you find joy, when things get tough

A good friend is patient, and always lends a hand
Their kindness and support, a source of comfort to stand
They listen with their heart, and understand
And offer a shoulder, to lend a helping hand

A good friend is trustworthy, and always keeps their word
Their loyalty and honesty, a treasure to be heard
They celebrate your triumphs, and help you through your pain
And offer a listening ear, when you need to explain

Best friends are the ones, who hold a special place
In our hearts and memories, with a smile on their face
They've been with us, through thick and thin
A constant companion, until the very end

Best friends are honest, and tell us like it is
Their words of wisdom, a priceless gift to give
They offer a listening ear, and a heart that understands
A source of comfort, in a world that often demands

Best friends are kind, and give without a thought
Their generosity, a treasure that cannot be bought
They lift us up, when we're feeling low
And stand by us, through the highs and the lows

Best friends are the ones, who know you inside and out
A constant companion, who'll never sell you out
They stand by your side, through thick and thin
And help you find joy, when life wears you thin

Best friends are loyal, and always there
Their love and support, a treasure beyond compare
They lift you up, when you're feeling down
And bring you peace, when life wears you out

Best friends are honest, and always speak the truth
Their words of wisdom, a guiding light for you
They offer a shoulder, to ease the pain
And help you find happiness, again and again

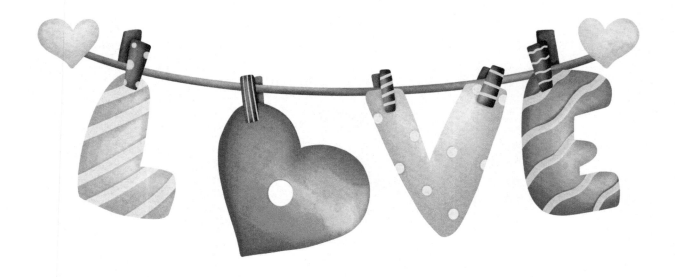

Best friends are the ones, who understand and care
A constant companion, who'll always be there
They know just what to say, and what to do
To lift us up, when we're feeling blue

Best friends are patient, and always lend a hand
Their kindness and support, a source of comfort to stand
They listen with their heart, and offer a shoulder to cry
A source of comfort, as we watch the world go by

Best friends are trustworthy, and keep our secrets safe
Their loyalty and honesty, a bond that can't be broken or erased
They celebrate our triumphs, and help us through our pain
A source of happiness, and sunshine through the rain

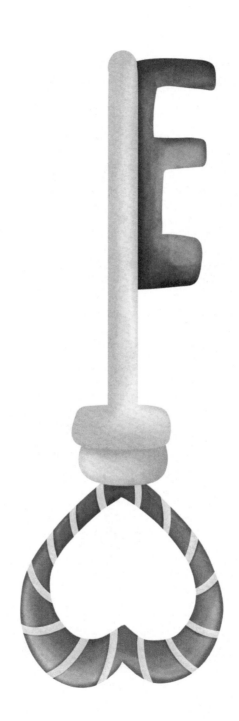

Friends in good times, bring laughter and light
A source of joy, in the day and the night
They lift us up, when our spirits are low
And help us find happiness, wherever we go

Friends in good times, share memories to last
The moments we cherish, forever they'll fast
In our hearts and our minds, they'll always remain
A source of comfort, in sunshine and rain

Friends in good times, make life worth the while
Their laughter and love, bring a constant smile
They offer a hand, when we need a friend
And help us find joy, that will never end

So here's to friends in good times, a bond so rare and bright
A treasure that shines, through the day and the night
For friends in good times, are a gift from above
A blessing to have, in a world filled with love.

Friends in good times, bring laughter and cheer
A source of happiness, throughout the year
They help us see the beauty, in life's simple things
And lift us up, when our hearts need healing

Friends in good times, create memories to last
The moments we cherish, forever they'll fast
In our hearts and our minds, they'll always remain
A source of comfort, through sunshine and rain

Friends in good times, share in our joy
Their laughter and love, a source of happiness to enjoy
They offer a shoulder, to lean on when we need
And help us find peace, and happiness indeed

So here's to friends in good times, a bond so bright and true
A treasure that shines, and shines anew
For friends in good times, are a gift from above
A blessing to have, in a world filled with love.

Friends in good times, bring joy to our days
A source of laughter, in many ways
They light up our world, with their warmth and their smile
And make life's journey, more worthwhile

Friends in good times, share memories so bright
The moments we cherish, forever in sight
In our hearts and our minds, they'll always remain
A source of comfort, through sunshine and rain

Friends in good times, bring comfort and care
A constant companion, always there
They offer a hand, when we need a friend
And help us find joy, that will never end

Friends in bad times, bring comfort and care
A constant companion, always there
They offer a shoulder, to lean on and cry
And help us find peace, as we watch the world go by

Friends in bad times, help us find our way
Their guidance and support, a source of strength each day
They listen with their heart, and offer a hand
Their kindness and love, a source of comfort to stand

Friends in bad times, share in our pain
Their empathy and love, ease the hurt and the strain
They celebrate our triumphs, and help us through our loss
A source of comfort, at any cost

Friends in bad times, bring hope in the dark
A source of comfort, to lighten the heart
They offer a hand, when we need a friend
And help us find peace, until the day's end

Friends in bad times, listen with their heart
Their understanding, a source of hope to impart
They share in our pain, and offer a smile
Their love and support, all the while

Friends in bad times, walk by our side
Their courage and strength, help us keep our stride
They lift us up, when our spirits are low
And help us find light, where shadows may grow

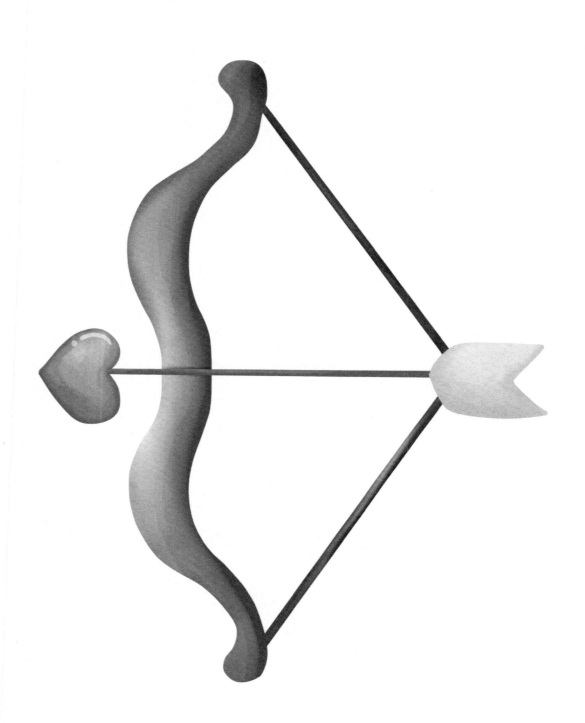

Friends in bad times, bring comfort and light
A source of hope, to guide us through the night
They offer a shoulder, to lean on and cry
And help us find peace, until the morning sky

Friends in bad times, help us stand tall
Their support and encouragement, helps us rise after a fall
They listen with their heart, and offer a hand
Their kindness and love, a source of comfort to withstand

Friends in bad times, share in our pain
Their empathy and love, helps ease the hurt and the strain
They celebrate our triumphs, and hold us through our loss
A source of comfort, at any cost

Friendship brings joy, to our lives each day
A source of happiness, in a world that may stray
It's a bond that is strong, and a light that shines bright
A treasure that brings, happiness day and night

Friendship brings laughter, to chase away the blues
A companion to share, all the things we love to do
It's a bond that is real, and a source of delight
A treasure that brings, happiness day and night

Friendship brings comfort, to soothe the weary soul
A source of solace, in a world that can be cold
It's a bond that is warm, and a light that shines bright
A treasure that brings, happiness day and night

Friendship brings joy, to our lives so bright
A source of laughter, on even the darkest night
It's a bond that is strong, and a light that shines true
A treasure that brings, happiness all the way through

Friendship brings laughter, and memories to share
A companion to cherish, through life's ups and downs everywhere
It's a bond that is real, and a source of great delight
A treasure that brings, happiness day and night

Friendship brings comfort, in times of need
A source of support, in life's moments of speed
It's a bond that is warm, and a light that shines bright
A treasure that brings, happiness day and night

Friendship brings joy, like a warm summer's breeze
A source of happiness, in life's struggles and squeezes
It's a bond that is strong, and a light that shines bright
A treasure that brings, happiness day and night

Friendship brings laughter, in times of play
A companion to cherish, through life's paths every day
It's a bond that is real, and a source of great joy
A treasure that brings, happiness to every girl and boy

Friendship brings comfort, in moments of pain
A source of solace, in life's troubles and strain
It's a bond that is warm, and a light that shines bright
A treasure that brings, happiness day and night

So here's to friendship, a bond so rare and divine
A treasure that brings, joy in a life that is thine
It's a gift from above, that we hold so dear
A blessing to have, in a world filled with cheer.

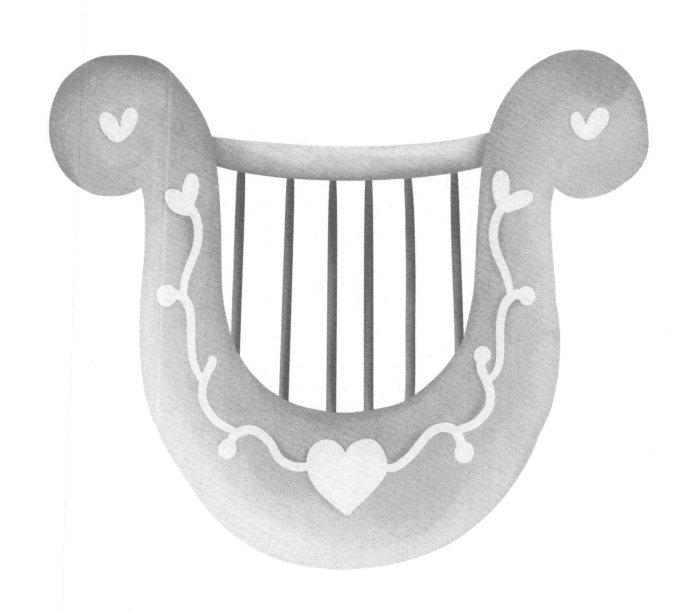

Challenges come, in every friendship's way
Tests of our bond, that we must face each day
But through thick and thin, our friendship will remain
A source of strength, through all life's joys and pains

We may argue, and say things we don't mean
Our feelings may hurt, and tempers may get lean
But through it all, our friendship will endure
A bond that's so strong, it will always be pure

There may be distance, that separates us for a while
Or life may bring changes, that test our friendship's smile
But through it all, our bond will remain steadfast
A friendship that will endure, until our very last

So here's to friendship, a bond so rare and true
A treasure that shines, through all life's challenges and due
With love and support, we will always overcome
Our friendship will thrive, and forever be young.

Challenges may come, like a storm in the night
Tests of our bond, that we must face with might
But through every trial, our friendship will hold
A source of comfort, in life's tales untold

We may disagree, and see things from different views
Our opinions may clash, and create an unease in our hues
But through it all, our friendship will persist
A bond that's unbreakable, with a love that won't miss

There may be moments, where we drift apart
Or life may bring changes, that test our friendship's heart
But through it all, our bond will remain steadfast
A friendship that will endure, and outlast

So here's to friendship, a bond so rare and bright
A treasure that shines, through all life's challenges and in sight
With open arms and hearts, we will always overcome
Our friendship will flourish, and forever be young.

Challenges may arise, like ripples in a stream
Tests of our bond, that we must face as a team
But through every storm, our friendship will stand
A source of courage, in life's shifting sands

We may falter, and stumble along the way
Our paths may diverge, and lead us astray
But through it all, our friendship will remain
A bond that's unbreakable, a love that will sustain

There may be hardships, that we must face alone
Or life may bring tests, that threaten to overthrow
But through it all, our bond will persist
A friendship that will endure, with a love that won't miss

So here's to friendship, a bond so rare and dear
A treasure that shines, through all life's challenges and year
With trust and understanding, we will always overcome
Our friendship will flourish, and forever be young.

For my friend, I wish so much happiness and peace
A heart filled with love, and life's worries at ease
A path that is bright, with no shadows in sight
A journey that brings, a smile to their light

I wish for them strength, in every challenge they face
The courage to stand, with a smile on their grace
The wisdom to choose, the right path to pursue
And the confidence to know, their dreams will come true

I wish for them joy, in every moment they live
The laughter that comes, from the life that they give
The love of their friends, and the comfort it brings
And the peace that comes, from the love that they sing

So here's to my friend, and the life that they lead
A journey that shines, with all that they need
With these wishes in heart, I send them my love
A treasure that shines, from heaven above.

For my friend, I wish a world of endless delight
A place where their laughter, will shine ever so bright
Where sunshine and rainbows, fill every day
And joy fills their heart, in every single way

I wish for them peace, in every step they take
The calmness of spirit, that they so richly make
A serenity that lasts, through every storm and strife
And a heart filled with love, for a lifetime of life

I wish for them dreams, that never fade away
And the courage to chase, each and every one that they may
The strength to believe, in their own power to grow
And the confidence to know, that they can achieve it all, don't you know

So here's to my friend, and the future they face
A journey of wonder, with a smile that they trace
With these wishes in heart, I send them my love
A treasure that shines, from heaven above.

For my friend, I wish a world of endless delight
Where their heart is filled, with love and delight
Where kindness and joy, are the gifts they receive
And peace is the treasure, they'll always retrieve

I wish for them strength, when life gets tough
The courage to rise, when the going gets rough
The resilience to endure, through every trial
And the wisdom to know, what's truly worthwhile

I wish for them friends, who'll walk by their side
And a love that will last, through thick and thin tides
A bond that is unbreakable, a treasure so rare
And a friendship that brings, a smile to their face everywhere

So here's to a friend, who brightens our days
With love and laughter, in so many ways
A person we cherish, with all of our hearts
A trusted companion, with whom we won't part.

Children so young, with hearts pure and bright
They find joy in laughter, and play that is light
Friends to each other, they bond in such glee
And share secrets and giggles, in innocence so free

They run through the fields, with arms open wide
Chasing each other, with joy as their guide
Their laughter echoing, in a symphony so sweet
And their bond growing stronger, with each and every treat

They build sandcastles, and climb trees so high
Exploring the world, with curious eyes and a sigh
Their friendship so simple, and pure in its ways
Bringing happiness and joy, to their childhood days

So here's to the children, and the bond that they share
A friendship so precious, beyond compare
With hearts so full of love, and laughter so loud
Their friendship will last, and always stand proud.

From childhood friends, to partners in life
A bond that lasts forever, through joy and strife
Growing old together, with memories so dear
Friends from the start, to the end of the year

They laugh and they play, through the years gone by
Holding hands together, as the world goes by
They share all their dreams, and all of their fears
And their bond only grows, with each passing year

They see each other through, the highs and the lows
Their friendship unbreakable, like a redwood tree grows
With love that is strong, and support that is true
Their bond lasts forever, with friendship so true

So here's to the friends, that last all life long
A bond so precious, worth more than gold and song
Together they grow old, with love that shines bright
A friendship so dear, that lasts through the night.

Friends from the start, to the end of the road
Their bond lasts forever, as strong as a toad
Growing up together, sharing their lives
Their friendship a treasure, that forever thrives

From playing in parks, to strolling in fields
Their laughter and love, forever it yields
Years pass by quickly, and they're grown up at last
Their friendship so strong, it outlasts the past

Together they walk, through the ups and the downs
Their bond ever steadfast, never wears or wears down
With love that is true, and memories so dear
Their friendship lasts forever, year after year

So here's to the friends, who've stood the test of time
A bond so precious, it shines like a rhyme
Together they grow old, with laughter and cheer
Their friendship so dear, that lasts all the year.

Friends from the start, till the end of the tale
A bond that lasts forever, a story so frail
Growing old together, through joy and through pain
Their friendship a treasure, that remains the same

From playing in sun, to walking in rain
Their bond always strong, it never wanes
Years go by quickly, but their love stays the same
Their friendship so dear, it bears their name

Together they stand, through thick and through thin
Their bond unbreakable, like a golden pin
With love that's unwavering, and memories so bright
Their friendship lasts forever, shining through the night

So here's to the friends, who've shared life's ride
A bond so precious, it glows like the tide
Together they grow old, with hearts full of glee
Their friendship so dear, it's meant to be.

Friends are like socks, they come in all sorts
Some are plain, some are wacky with shorts
They keep us warm, and make us smile
They're with us for miles and miles

Friends are like monkeys, always on the go
They love to play and put on a show
They swing from vines, and climb up high
And make us laugh, until we cry

Friends are like pizza, always there for you
They come in all shapes, and toppings too
Some are spicy, some are sweet
They always make your day complete

So here's to friends, who bring us joy
They fill our hearts, with laughter and poise
Together we laugh, and dance in the sun
Our friendship so funny, it's second to none!

Friends are like balloons, they lift us so high
With laughter and giggles, they fill up the sky
They bounce and they float, with a twirl and a twist
Their joy is contagious, it can't be missed

Friends are like music, they bring us to life
With melodies sweet, and a beat that's so right
They fill up the room, with laughter and cheer
Their rhythm so contagious, it's hard not to hear

Friends are like candy, so sweet and so bright
With colors so vivid, they light up the night
They come in all shapes, and sizes too
And always make our day, brighter and new

So here's to friends, who bring us so much fun
With laughter and joy, they are second to none
Together we dance, and sing in the sun
Our friendship so funny, it's just begun!

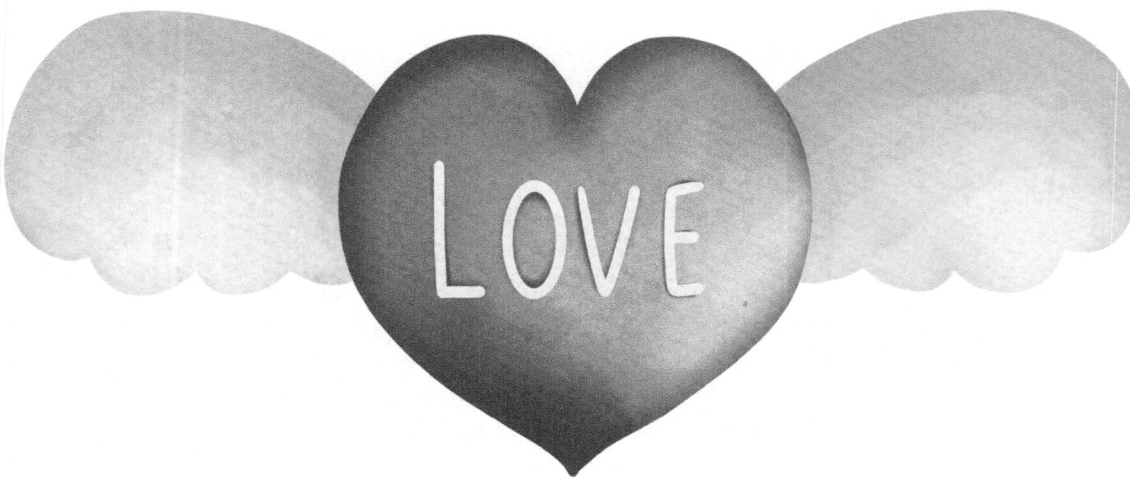
LOVE

Friends are like rubber bands, they stretch and they bend
With laughter and giggles, they never come to an end
They hold us tight, and never let go
With jokes and pranks, they keep us aglow

Friends are like sunshine, they brighten our day
With warmth and kindness, they chase the grey away
They shine so bright, and bring us delight
Their joy is so infectious, it's hard to fight

Friends are like jokes, they always get the punch
With giggles and laughter, they bring us to lunch
They tickle our funny bone, and make us smile
Their humor so contagious, it's worth every mile

So here's to friends, who bring us so much joy
With laughter and humor, they are simply a joy
Together we laugh, and dance in the sun
Our friendship so funny, it's just begun!